Navigating Choices, With Purpose

A Teen And Young Adult Guide
For Making Reasoned And
Purposeful Choices.

By

Tasha R. Famuyiwa

© **Copyright 2018. Tasha R. Famuyiwa**

Unless otherwise indicated, all scripture quotations are taken from the HOLY BIBLE, NEW INTERNATIONAL VERSION®, NIV® Copyright © 1973, 1978, 1984, 2011 by Biblica, Inc.® Used by permission. All rights reserved worldwide.

No part of this publication may be reproduced, stored in a retrieval system, or transmitted in any form or by any means, electronic, mechanical, photocopying or otherwise, without the prior permission of the copyright owner.

ISBN: 9780692071977

ALL RIGHTS RESERVED

Printed in the U.S.A.

Acknowledgement

First and foremost, I would like to thank my heavenly Father for his unconditional love, grace and mercy.

I would also like to thank my husband who inspires me through his perseverance, his strength, his love for Christ, and his love for me.

I would also like to thank my mother, who has been a light for me in my darkest days.

And I want to thank my siblings for accepting me for me.

Table of Contents

Part I: Factors That Influence the Choices We Make 1

Chapter 1: Who's To Blame?........................ 2

Chapter 2: The Danger Of Choosing To Be Neutral.. 10

Chapter 3: Why Did I Change My Mind? 18

Chapter 4: How Our Emotions Impact Our Choices.. 23

Chapter 5: Our Values Impact Our Choices.. 31

Chapter 6: The Cycle Of Past Generational Choices.. 38

Chapter 7: Society Influences Our Choices.. 43

Chapter 8: Ways Our Peers Influence Our Choices.. 49

Part II: Ways We Can Make Better Choices 55

Chapter 9: Take The Leap Of Faith 58

Chapter 10: Check Your Self...................... 64

Chapter 11: Don't Rush 69

Chapter 12: Stop Comparing Yourself To Others.. 74

Chapter 13: Look At The Big Picture 78

Chapter 14: Seek Advice 84

Chapter 15: Keep Choosing The Right Way Until It Becomes A Natural Response..... 88

Chapter 16: Be Mindful Of Others 96

Chapter 17: Learn From Past Mistakes And Experiences... 102

Final Chapter God's Grace...................... 105

References 109

Part I
Factors That Influence the Choices We Make

Chapter 1
Who's to Blame?

Looking out to the streets as cars passed by in the Florida heat was not how I wanted to spend the rest of my afternoon on a school night. My twin sister and I missed the school bus and had no choice but to take the city bus home. Unlike the school bus, which stopped about two blocks from our house, the city bus stopped about two-and-a-half miles away from home, which meant I had to hear my sister complain and remind me how hot it was for the next hour. Fed up and tired, my sister put out her arm and stuck her thumb up in an effort to hitch a ride home. At first I just laughed and tried to stop her before someone really stopped their car for us, but as we walked she continued to hold her arm out.

Hoping no one would stop for us, I began to walk a little faster, thinking my sister would just give up and begin walking faster as well. But then I heard the sound of tires slowing down on the pavement behind us. Taking a deep breath, I looked back to see my sister looking into the car as if she had just struck gold. My sister opened the door and waited for me as I walked toward the car, because she knew I was not going to let her hitch a ride alone.

As soon as I reached the car, I immediately began to panic; the driver was this huge older guy who looked like he could easily take the both of us out. My sister and I were about sixteen years old at the time, and the guy looked like he was in his mid-forties. We both sat in the back seat, and my sister began to tell the guy where to drop us off. As she was talking, I was looking for ways to escape if he tried to kidnap us. I was looking at the doors, the windows, and how fast he was driving just in case we had to jump out of his moving car. My sister, on the other hand, seemed so relaxed as she kept talking and answering all of the guy's questions. She did not appear to be worried at all.

Looking back, I can't believe that I actually got into the car of a stranger. Knowing all that I know today, I would have never allowed myself or my sister to get into that car. That was by far the riskiest decision I ever made in my teenage years. Fortunately for us, the guy did not try anything out of the ordinary; he dropped us off at our stop and drove away. But if anything bad had happened to us, we would have been to blame, because at the end of the day, it was our choice to get into his car.

Throughout my life there have been countless times I made similar uncalculated, risky, and foolish decisions. And each time, whether I came out on the other side safe without a scratch, or hurt and wounded, I knew there was no one to blame but myself, because when it was all said and done, it was my choice.

Yes, my choice.

The Oxford Dictionary defines choice as an act of choosing between two or more possibilities, the right or ability to choose. Not the most reliable source, but I like how Wikipedia defines choice, as an act that involves decision making, which includes judging the merits of multiple options and selecting one or more of them. One can make a choice between imagined options ("What would I do if...?") or between real options followed by the corresponding action.

I learned a valuable lesson the day my sister and I hitched a ride home: that although we make crazy and unwise decisions at times, we have a Savior who will get in the car with us and begin to think of ways to set us free if anything were to happen to us. We have a Friend who not only will warn us of danger, but also will be there every step of the way to ensure our safety. I'm talking about a Friend named Jesus. My concern for my sister's safety was just a shadow of how God is concerned for us even when we knowingly put ourselves in harm's way.

Making bold decisions and taking risks was definitely a trait my siblings and I inherited from our mother. My mother was only 20 years old when she made one of the biggest decisions of her life; she decided to migrate from Haiti to the United States in August, 1980. I remember growing up and asking my mother what made her decide to move to America; she would laugh and say, "I thought the streets were made of gold." But underneath her smile, I could see her desperation to know if she had made the right choice. My mother became a widow in 1996, but already lived as a single parent before then. My father was in and out of jail for most of my life. He did anything and everything to try to keep a roof over our heads and food on the table—including stealing. My father's choices were much different from my mother's. She decided to go to church every day of the week in search of peace.

Although I was young and may not have understood much back then, I knew life was hard for my mother. I would wake up in the middle of the night and hear my mother crying. I knew she didn't want us to see her cry, so I would just lie on the bed I shared with four of my sisters and try to force myself back to sleep, as she cried throughout the night. For my mother, the American dream was still but a dream. However, not once did I ever see her quit or give up, because my mother knew that for every choice she made she had to live with the outcome. I watched my mother wake up every morning and choose to live every day the best she could, not just for her kids, but also for herself. Every day I watched my mother make the decision to keep moving forward and never give up.

Making decisions is a part of life, and each decision can bring us closer to our heavenly Father and His plans for our life—or it can take us further away from our destiny.

In the scriptures, there is a story about the first human beings to walk the earth, Adam and Eve, and the choice they made in the Garden of Eden. The Lord told Adam and Eve not to eat fruit grown from a specific tree. God had given Adam the option to eat from all the other trees in the garden except for one. As it is written, "You are free to eat from any tree in the garden; but you must not eat from the tree of the knowledge of good and evil, for when you eat from it you will certainly die" (Gen. 2:16–17).

The serpent tempted Eve into eating the fruit, which she later convinced Adam to eat. I have read and heard this story countless times, and every time the story of Adam and Eve is preached in a sermon or written in a book, it highlights the downfall of humanity. However, when I read this story I think to myself, why would God put a tree in the middle of the garden if he did not want Adam and Eve to eat from it? Then it dawned on me that the God of the universe allows humankind to make their own decisions.

The Creator of everything has given each of us the power of free will and the power to make our own choices. Throughout the Bible the Lord gave people instructions and commandments to obey; however, God never once took away anyone's free will to follow Him.

In Deuteronomy chapter 30, the Lord says to the children of Israel, "This day I call the heavens and the earth as witnesses against you that I have set before you life and death, blessings and curses. Now choose life, so that you and your children may live" (Deut. 30:19).

In this verse I notice the instruction is written clearly, and two options are presented. I also realize that power has been transferred from God to the children of Israel, the power of free will. That is our power, the power to choose. I have the power to choose to forgive, to love, to hate, to run, or to stay. Every choice we make will affect the way we live, and it is critical that we make choices that bring power and light to our destiny.

I have the privilege of working with teenagers and young adults, and over the years I have witnessed many of the youth stray from their parents' teaching and faith, only to come to the realization that the grass is not always greener on the other side. For some, the experience was an eye opener; for others the shame and guilt was too much to return to a place of normalcy. But thank God, nothing can separate us from His love.

Often I hear young celebrities say that they will "have it all figured out" in their thirties, as if the choices they make while they're young will have no repercussions or lasting effect. But no one is ever too young to start living a life that can leave a positive impact on the world.

My hope is that this book will enlighten you to make choices that bring life. Each day is a gift, and it is important that we become better stewards of this gift by making choices that will benefit not only ourselves, but those around us.

It is with great honor that I invite you to come along with me and explore the impact our choices have on our future.

Chapter 2
The Danger of Choosing to Be Neutral

Our surroundings, our upbringing, and the media shape our perspective of issues that arise in our society. We are living in a time when we can connect to people all over the world through the internet, social media, and the news. However, factors such as race, religion, and class influence how we might view a social problem differently from our peers based on their particular frame of reference, a process known as "selective perception." We all can choose or select what is important to us and what isn't. These factors also impact how we relate to one another emotionally and physically.

I remember having lunch with a co-worker who was born in India. She moved to America to attend college, and later went through the process of becoming a permanent resident with the help of her older sister who had married an American citizen. We would occasionally eat lunch together because I wanted to get to know more about her and her culture. One day I asked her if there was racism in India. She said, "No, not like here, but there is tension between different religious groups, which I guess you can compare to racism." She went on to say that, "Many people have died because of their religious preference in India." Not knowing how to respond to her statement, we both ate in silence for a minute or two, and then we began to talk about other topics like recipes for Indian cuisine and our favorite food.

After a while our conversation returned to religion and race. While I took a bite of my sandwich, she said, "Before I came to America many people warned me about racism." She went on, "I was told to choose to side with white Americans as opposed to African Americans." Again the room grew silent because at that moment my mind was trying to process the emotion I was experiencing. Smiling, she said, "But I'm not like that," and explained that her niece is actually mixed and her brother-in-law is black. Feeling a little more relaxed, we began to talk about our family and our upbringing, but for the rest of our conversation I could not help but wonder why someone would tell her to choose a side when it comes to racism. Instead, I would think her family and friends would have advised her to remain neutral. Then I thought to myself, could someone really remain neutral about racism or religious oppression? And then I remembered a quote from Martin Luther King, Jr., when he said, "In the end, we will remember not the words of our enemies but the silence of our friends." You can choose to fight for equality or not fight at all. But in the decision to not fight at all, you have actually made your choice.

For a long time I believed that my decision to remain neutral on certain topics was the wise thing to do. I grew up in a household with nine siblings and was born with an outspoken twin, as I mentioned earlier. And if anyone knows both my twin and me, they would describe our personalities as night and day. I consider myself to be quiet and calm with a strong inner sense of self-awareness, meaning I try to analyze the situation before letting my emotions get the best of me.

On the other hand, my twin is loud, outspoken, funny, dramatic, and extremely sensitive. Whenever arguments would come up at our house, which was quite often, I would just stay quiet and wait for someone to make the final decision. When one of my siblings would ask for my input, I would look around the room and try to make a statement that would not offend either side. In many cases, my twin would roll her eyes, interrupt me in the middle of my response, and make the decision for me. It was in those moments I realized that choosing to be neutral is disgusting.

A verse from the Book of Revelation states, "Because you are lukewarm—neither hot nor cold—I am about to spit you out of my mouth" (Rev. 3:16).

The idea of choosing to be neutral has a bad aftertaste. It first sounds sweet and understanding, but then leaves people around you frustrated because you never really make a choice. It seems no matter how hard I tried not to upset anyone by remaining neutral, I would still find myself offending someone.

However, society has made it difficult to make solid choices for fear of being offensive. The term "politically correct" describes language, policies, or measures that are intended not to offend or disadvantage any particular group of people in society. The notion of political correctness can influence how we make choices, and for someone like myself, choosing to be indifferent seems like the only way out.

Controversial topics such as abortion, homosexuality, and religious freedom are usually analyzed from a politically correct viewpoint, which encompasses an idea of neutrality or measures that are not intended to offend any particular group.

A high school student I tutored in the summer of 2016 was a free-spirited teenage boy attending a private Catholic high school that he hated. He would tell me that he was not religious and that he felt disconnected from his school friends. In one of our conversations he explained how unhappy he was at school because he felt he was being labeled as something he did not identify himself to be. I often hear people make similar remarks when asked why they can't make a decision on a certain topic—because no one wants to be labeled or confined.

Our resistance to being labeled creates an attitude of neutrality, which can be detrimental to our identity. It would be pretty difficult to describe yourself using a phrase such as, "I think I am indifferent." I still remember back in college how people would suddenly change their behavior whenever I came around them, because many people knew I was a Christian, and they labeled me as someone that they could not be themselves around. At first I used to get so confused and frustrated, because I felt like an outsider. I would try everything to make people believe that I was not that type of person. In my effort to be more acceptable, I began to lose who I was and what I stood for. My "no" became "probably" and my "yes" became "I'm not sure." I was beginning to notice that every time I chose to remain neutral, and allow society, my environment, or my twin sister to make the choice for me, I felt as if I was not being true to myself. Alexander Hamilton said, "If you don't stand for something, you'll fall for anything." In a time such as this, our choices define us. By remaining silent on subjects that were important to me, I began to feel unsure about who I was as an individual.

I know some of you might be reading this and say it is easier said than done to "let your yes be yes and your no be no." I wish it could be that simple in an ever-changing world. History has proven that societal norms are forever changing, and some things that are forbidden today might become totally acceptable tomorrow, so choosing to be neutral might seem like the only way out.

The women's liberation movement, commonly known as the feminist movement, can be traced back to the first women's rights convention held in Seneca Falls, New York in 1848. Elizabeth Cady and Lucretia Mott organized the meeting to discuss social, civil, and religious conditions and rights of women.

These women were way ahead of their time since women were not even allowed to vote in the 1800s. Back then women had little to no voice in society, were not allowed an education, and were not given the same opportunities men were given. It was forbidden for women to hold any political position, nor were they allowed to enjoy financial and educational freedom. The advancement of women in America was made possible by Elizabeth Cady and other courageous men and women who signed the Declaration of Sentiments in 1848, a document which helped women attain their rights.

Yes, you read that correctly: men contributed to the advancement of women's rights in America. The Declaration of Sentiments was signed by sixty-eight women and thirty-two men. The men who signed the declaration did not sit around and choose to be neutral against women's inequality; instead they were bold by signing their names to show that they agreed with the advancement of women.

Change can only happen if we step out of our neutral comfort zone and begin to make bold, firm choices, even against societal norms. My point is that there isn't a box we can check for "neutral." Life simply does not present neutral options. You are either going to choose yes or no, left or right, good or bad, life or death; so I encourage you to choose life in everything you do. The decision to choose life simply means to choose to live in a way that brings joy and fulfillment to you and others around you: a life that is pleasing to our heavenly Father.

Chapter 3
Why Did I Change My Mind?

Have you ever asked yourself, why did I change my answer? [Or] Why did I buy this pair of pants instead of the ones I wanted originally? [Or] Why did I not stick to my decision to go back to school? We've all changed our minds one time or another. For some, changing our mind was the best decision we made, and for others it may have been the worst.

I have the privilege of working in both of the fields I majored in. I received a bachelor's degree in sociology, with a minor in accounting at the University of Florida, and went on to receive a master's degree in accounting at Florida Atlantic University. I enjoy working as an accountant in the daytime and working with children and adolescent teens in the foster care system in the evening. However, I sometimes wonder what would have become of me if I did not change my mind—if I had stuck to my first career choice.

I originally wanted to be a news reporter. I remember freshman year orientation at the

University of Florida when all the students got the chance to learn more about each major offered there. Without any hesitation, I went straight into the room where a teaching assistant was giving a presentation about the College of Journalism and Communications. Looking at the brochure and the requirements for graduation, I began to reconsider a career path as a journalist. At eighteen years of age, there could have been numerous reasons I decided to change my mind, like not feeling pretty enough as I compared myself to the photo on the brochure, or not feeling qualified. Whatever thought process led me to reconsider majoring in journalism came from a place of feeling intimidated. Timid is the root word of intimidate, which derives from the Latin intimidatus, meaning "to make afraid." One definition of intimidate is "to force into or deter from some action by inducing fear." I changed my mind out of fear. It took me a while to realize that fear has been the underlying factor the majority of the times I decided to change my mind. Where could this feeling of fear have originated?

"For God has not given us a spirit of fear, but of power and of love and of a sound mind" (2 Tim. 1:7) NKJV.

Therefore, I realized that if I could eliminate fear, I would be able to have a sound mind when making a decision.

Some of you may doubt whether fear was truly the underlying reason I decided to change my mind. Maybe it was simply a conscious decision. Every day we make choices, subconsciously or well thought out. And sometimes life itself can change the course of our direction, which can still leave us asking, "what if?".

One conversation I had with a co-worker helped me better understand the impact of changing a decision. While working toward my master's degree, I had a front desk receptionist job at a condominium complex in Fort Lauderdale. My co-worker was the condominium's accountant. She seemed to have her life together—nice car, well dressed, great personality. She took me under her wing and mentored me in networking and building a brand for myself. We worked really well together. I began to open up to her about my personal life and told her about my boyfriend at the time (now my husband), and she began to open up to me, too. While we were eating lunch together she advised me with a stern look on her face, "When you get married to your husband, do not wait too long to have kids." She had decided to marry her longtime boyfriend at the age of twenty-seven. She and her husband wanted to start a family right away, but she decided not to have kids at that time so she could focus on her career. After five years of marriage she felt ready to have kids, but found out her husband was unfaithful to her, so she made the tough decision to get a divorce.

After her divorce she remarried and was ready to have kids right away, but struggled to get pregnant. After two years of trying, she conceived, but lost the child. I still remember the somber look on her face as she sat across the table from me, at age fifty-six, telling me she wished she had had kids sooner with her first husband.

Our choices can bring life or death. Sometimes we feel that we are making the best decision when we actually go against what God has planned for our lives. But in the end we look back trying to see what we could have done differently. Choosing a different path than the one we originally planned may result from our own reasoning, but sometimes it is due to God's intervention.

A 9/11 survivor told a news reporter that he decided at the last minute not to take a fishing trip with his uncle. Changing his mind saved his life; the plane he was scheduled to fly on was the one that crashed into the Pentagon on September 11, 2001.

Having a change of mind when making a decision is perfectly okay. Just understand that whatever choice we settle on, there is a corresponding choice we have foregone. Michael Josephson once said, "Choices you make in life will make your life, so choose wisely." When all is said and done, we are a product of both the choices we make and the choices we have foregone.

Chapter 4
How Our Emotions Impact Our Choices

Our emotions and instincts are controlled by the amygdala. The amygdala is a small part of the brain located in the temporal lobe. The amygdala controls our reflexes to danger and is able to process a ton of information within milliseconds. When a person becomes angry, blood rushes through the frontal cortex, clouding rational behavior. The feeling of anger increases our blood pressure and heart rate, and increases cortisol, a stress hormone. The feeling of anger causes the left hemisphere of the brain to become more stimulated. Anger is a negative emotion, but it should not be suppressed. In fact it's okay to get angry sometimes; it's our resulting actions that we must be careful about. We should be "quick to listen, slow to speak, and slow to become angry" (James 1:19).

It is important not to act or make important decisions based on emotions alone. I have read and heard so many stories in the news, or from friends and family, of ruined relationships and great opportunities lost because they could not control their emotions.

I never considered myself an emotional person, which has helped me in some areas of my life. However, I notice that certain feelings come easier to me than others, like jealousy, pride, even hate. Unconsciously, I gravitate towards negative emotions and find myself having to seriously pray and consciously try to think and feel positively about myself and others around me.

Research has found that negative thoughts and emotions are more contagious and have a greater impact than positive emotions; this is known as negative bias. Researchers are studying whether humans are wired to construct negative emotions more readily than positive emotions. Whatever the research shows, I believe that we have the ability to choose and control our emotions, thus allowing us to have some clarity when making decisions.

Whitney Houston's famous song, "Why Does it Hurt So Bad?" speaks of the emotional pain she felt after losing someone she loved. Some people have said emotional pain feels worse than physical pain and in some cases lasts longer as well. An article titled, "5 Ways Emotional Pain is Worse than Physical Pain[1]" lists reasons why emotional pain can be more damaging to the body than physical pain. The second reason was the most alarming to me, as it states that people will often "use physical pain as a distraction from emotional pain, not vice versa." To cope with emotional pain, some people inflict self-injury, and some even choose to end their lives over momentary emotional pain.

I urge anyone whoever reads this book to never make a critical decision like committing suicide based on fleeting emotions; instead we should base our decisions on truth and the Word of God. "Weeping may stay for the night, but rejoicing comes in the morning" (Psalms 30:5).

The way we feel about our present circumstances impacts how we make future choices. I remember vividly my older sister yelling at my mother about not being able to afford basic things other teenagers' parents could. She would shout, "I did not choose to be born into this family!" and I would watch

---

[1] Winch, Guy. "5 Ways Emotional Pain Is Worse Than Physical Pain." Psychology Today, Sussex Publishers, 20 July 2014,

my mother quietly walk away into her room as my older sister continued to complain. I knew my mother would have given us the world if she could. There are some things in life that we did not choose to happen to us, like being born into poverty, and although some of those things can be very difficult to escape, we do have the choice to either remain victims of our circumstances or become victors. Maya Angelou once said, "You may not control all the events that happen to you, but you can decide not to be reduced by them."

Maya Angelou is considered one of the greatest poets of the twenty-first century. Maya was born in 1928 in St. Louis, Missouri, during a time of segregation, and when African Americans owned very little. At age seven, Maya was raped by her mother's boyfriend and was hospitalized. After Maya's abuser was let out of jail, he was found dead. Maya blamed herself for the murder of her rapist and decided not to speak for the next five years. During those five years Maya read all the books from the public library in the "black" neighborhood and read all the books she could get from the "white" school library. She began to memorize Shakespeare and poetry from other famous poets; this would mark the beginning of her successful career as an author and poet. Maya once said that "out of evil there can come good." At age fourteen Maya dropped out of high school, but she later returned and graduated, giving birth to her son weeks after her graduation.

Living through and overcoming the traumatic experience of rape, the psychological abuse of racism, and the struggles of poverty, Maya Angelou made a decision not to be reduced by her circumstances. She went on to write several books, recited one of her poems at the inauguration of President Clinton, and received the Presidential Medal of Freedom along with many others prestigious awards. She, like many other great men and women, decided not to let her circumstances control her destiny, her dream, and her purpose. I'm sure it was not an easy process for Maya to unravel and discard the way she viewed herself as a young child. It probably took several years for her to become the person we know today. Her decision to change her outlook on her life, her circumstance, and her self-image may have been the most important choice she ever made, and we all have the ability to make that choice in our own lives as well.

The way you see yourself—or your self-esteem, which is "a person's overall subjective emotional evaluation of his or her own worth"—can impact decisions you make. A news article titled, "14 Psychological Reasons Why Good People Do Bad Things[2]" written by Muel Kaptin explains how one can reason with him or herself into doing immoral acts.

One of the psychological reasons that caught my attention is known as the Galatea effect, which examines how self-image determines behavior. The Galatea effect suggests that people with a strong self-identity are less likely to commit fraud than those who possess a poor image of themselves, because they feel less responsible.

I suffered from a poor image of myself for a very long time. I still remember only eating a small amount of lettuce before working out for hours in the gym until I would throw up and faint from exhaustion. The way I viewed myself began to have a negative impact on the choices I was making in school and in my personal life. It took years for me to realize that

---

[2] Kaptein, Muel, Why Do Good People Sometimes Do Bad Things?: 52 Reflections on Ethics at Work (July 25, 2012).

I was created in the image of God (Gen. 1:27). I know it might sound cliché, but the moment I decided to change my thoughts and how I felt about myself, my life began to change as well.

Please do not assume that now I walk around feeling great about myself every day. I sometimes find myself overcoming one negative emotion by being absorbed by another one that is equally destructive. For instance, I would conquer self-esteem issues by becoming prideful or envious, leading to a cycle of bad choices. Pride and envy are interesting emotions in the way they can drive us to do great works, but also cause us to lose everything we work for. Solomon wrote in Ecclesiastes, "And I saw that all toil and all achievement spring from one person's envy of another. This too is meaningless, a chasing after the wind" (Eccles. 4:4).

To think that being envious of someone can lead to achieving great success is intriguing. Our feelings should not be ignored, as they can be important factors in our decision making, but they should not be the sole source of our reasoning when we are in the process of making important choices.

It is important to understand that our emotions and feelings are not just some abstract experience that happens to us. We have the ability to choose how we feel about others and how we feel about ourselves. When asked what the greatest commandment was, Jesus answered, "'Love the Lord your God with all your heart and with all your soul and with all your mind.' This is the first and greatest commandment. And the second is like it: 'Love your neighbor as yourself'" (Matt. 22:37–39).

Unlike other emotions mentioned in this chapter, love is a choice but also a command. My love for God and for others is the foundation of the choices I make in life, and in many ways, has helped me to make good decisions. I choose to operate on the emotion of love when making both small and big decisions.

Chapter 5
Our Values Impact Our Choices

My husband stated at one of his leadership conferences that the most valuable resource on earth is people. I know without a doubt that my husband values people by the choices he makes. Most of our arguments are about how much time he spends helping and caring for others, especially family and friends.

Roy E. Disney, the brother of Walt Disney, once said that "when your values are clear to you, making decisions becomes easier." Our values will have an impact on the choices we make. For most of us, the problem is trying to hold on to our values while still trying to be adaptable and relevant in society.

My mother's style of discipline has changed over the years. I can still remember my mother asking me to get a belt so she could beat my brother when he would bring her a bad report card. Now my mother doesn't even tap her grandson when he brings home a bad report card. Rather, she talks to him and tells him to stop watching TV for some time. Although my mother's style of discipline has changed, her appreciation for education remains the same. I once read a quote which says it's okay to "open your arms to change, but don't let go of your values."

Our values are an important attribute in our identity and the way we choose to live. Our values in many ways are the compass we use to navigate through life. Before there was electronic GPS, captains of ships would rely on manual tools like compasses to get to their destinations. A handheld compass simply tells you the direction you are heading, measured in degrees relative to magnetic north. The compass enables you to determine the direction in which the ship should sail. Our values and beliefs work in a similar way, in that our values determine the way we want to live, and our decisions help us achieve our goals.

Maslow's hierarchy of needs is a theory which defines basic human needs using a pyramid diagram. The bottom of the pyramid shows the most important basic needs, known as our physiological needs—in other words, the physical needs for survival including food, shelter, water, air, and clothing. If the physiological needs are not met, the subject is unlikely to survive.

The 2008 recession caused by the financial crisis was described as "the worst recession to hit America since the Great Depression." During the recession many lost their jobs, homes, and businesses. The collapse of the housing market caused thousands of homes to go into foreclosure, increasing the development of tent cities all across America. People had to adjust to a new way of living, and things they once considered important no longer were.

I remember having a conversation with my roommate in college during the recession; she confided in me how hard it was for her to stay focused on school because her house was in foreclosure. Having been through a similar situation, I tried to offer some advice and encouragement. She began to tell me more about her house which she shared with her sister and brothers and her mother. I learned that she lived in a very large house in an upscale community. As she continued to pour out her feelings to me, I could not stop myself from wondering why her mother, as a single parent, chose to purchase such a large house in a prestigious neighborhood. Her mother's decision to purchase the house my roommate grew up in could have been for numerous reasons, such as better schools, low crime rate, and network opportunities. Whatever the reason, perhaps the cost of the house should have been given more consideration.

After the conversation I had with my roommate, I realized that our values can impact many areas of our lives, even affecting how we spend money. I knew firsthand how my family and I struggled to make it through each day, so for me security has always been a major factor in my decision making. I would easily choose to forego living lavishly for living with the knowledge of my family's security.

For many of us, our values come from our religious communities or our family and friends; for others, values are developed through life experiences. Various events, people, and organizations have shaped my own values and beliefs.

In my freshman year in high school I took a sex education class. It was the longest hour of my life as my teacher showed the class videos and pictures of people who contracted sexually transmitted diseases. I believe the class was meant to instill fear in the students about having unprotected sex. The majority of my friends were, in fact, engaging in unprotected sex, which leads to unplanned pregnancies and—yes—sexually transmitted diseases.

Our society in many ways has devalued sex and its true meaning and purpose. Sex is a beautiful, spiritual expression of love between a husband and wife. It is also a blood covenant that is meant to seal an everlasting relationship between a man and a woman. Scripture tells us in Mark chapter 10, "At the beginning of creation God 'made them male and female.' 'For this reason a man will leave his father and mother and be united to his wife, and the two will become one flesh.' So they are no longer two, but one flesh. Therefore what God has joined together, let no one separate" (Mark 10:6–9).

It's easy to read a scripture like that and forget the true value of love and sex because of our constant exposure to society's norms and values. An article in the Huffington Post titled, "How Many Sexual Partners is Too Many?[3]" asserts that anyone with more than ten sexual partners is considered to be too promiscuous. We must be careful not to live and make decisions based on the world's standards. And for anyone who may have had a sexual relationship before marriage, please know that you are forgiven, but "sin no more," meaning don't continue to make

---

[3] Lo, Em &. "How Many Sexual Partners Is Too Many?" *The Huffington Post*, TheHuffingtonPost.com

choices that will jeopardize your physical, mental, and spiritual health.

Each individual life is a reflection of all the choices that person has made. My first journal quoted the Serenity Prayer in the front of the journal, and I would read it every time I opened it: "God grant me the serenity to accept the things I cannot change; courage to change the things I can; and wisdom to know the difference." The Serenity Prayer is used in drug rehab centers all across America to help patients realize that they have the ability to break free from their addictions. The goal of drug rehab centers is to help their patients stop drug abuse and "return them to productive functioning people in their family, workplace, and community." Most drug addicts turn from their addictions after leaving rehab centers, though many suffer from related health issues, while some are faced with the loss of friends and family members, and the lost time they can never get back.

Restoration and healing is a beautiful thing to witness, but the lingering thought of "how my life would have turned out if I had never…" Well, you can fill in the blank. Jim Rohn once said, "We must all suffer one of two things: the pain of discipline or the pain of regret." Our values should direct us to live a life that will bring us good and not harm, to not only ourselves, but also everyone around us. The truth is that we all might have different values; we all come from different walks of life. My hope is that we take time to assess our values to determine if our values are allowing us to make good, purposeful choices.

Chapter 6
The Cycle of Past Generational Choices

Taking the city bus to college is common in Gainesville, Florida. The majority of the students were on a first name basis with the bus drivers. I, on the other hand, did not really engage in conversation with any of the bus drivers, but there was this one bus driver who always spoke to me whenever I got on his bus. He looked much younger than the other drivers and really did not talk much with the college kids, except for me, for some reason. In one of our conversations he told me that his father and grandfather were both bus drivers in Puerto Rico and that he never wanted to become a bus driver. His dream was to get a college degree in business. I responded, "You're young, it's not too late," as if I just helped him solve all his problems. Without a word he turned to me, smirking, and shrugged his shoulder as if shaking off an impossible idea.

The choices our father and mother made in life do not have to be the same choices we make.

Yet it's not uncommon to hear, "My father was a doctor, and that's why I chose to be a doctor" or "my mother was a nurse, and that is why I am a nurse."

It's natural to acquire some of the same traits our parents have. Some traits that pass from one generation to the next can be beneficial for us, while other traits can be extremely harmful for our future and people around us.

The story of Cyntoia Brown, a sixteen-year-old charged with first degree murder in 2004, made me realize the cycle of poor choices can be passed on from one generation to the next; some may even call it generational curses. Cyntoia Brown was raised by her foster parents, but still found herself following the same path as her biological mother. Her case was distinctive in that it highlighted Cyntoia's personality disorder she acquired from her biological mother and through various traumatic experiences. Cyntoia's mother conceived her at the age of sixteen, the same age Cyntoia was when convicted of murder. In court, Cyntoia's biological mother explained the history of suicide in her family and how she suffers from depression and suicidal thoughts. In a recorded conversation with her psychiatrist, Cyntoia explained how depressed she was, and the events that took place in her life that led her to kill the man she had been paid to sleep with.

It is easier to look at someone and say that the individual choice was simply his or her own decision, but that is not always the case. Research has shown that those who suffer from suicidal thoughts, domestic violence, drug abuse, and alcoholism can trace similar behaviors and mental conditions from previous generations. It is important to understand that we are not our ancestors' mistakes and that we can break the cycle of poor choices and generational curses. In 2 Corinthians 5:17 it says, "Therefore, if anyone is in Christ, the new creation has come: the old has gone, the new is here!"

Working with kids in the foster care system, I get to witness firsthand patterns of bad choices passed from one generation to the next. At the home of one of my students, I saw four generations of women all sitting together in the kitchen; each woman had her first child before her twentieth birthday, and I was enjoying the conversation they were having among themselves. I could not help but notice my student, who was thirteen, texting her boyfriend a heart emoji, and I thought to myself, "will she follow in her mother's and grandmother's footsteps as well?"

Some of us grow up to become nothing like our fathers and mothers, either out of an attitude of rebellion or through prayer and wise counsel. It is not uncommon to hear the young boys in foster care that I tutor say, "I am never going to be like my dad." Most of the young men choose a different path than their fathers out of resentment, which I found to be very destructive in the choices these men make later in life.

In order to make better choices for ourselves and for our kids, we must first learn how to forgive our parents for the bad choices they made, and this can only be done through prayer and wise counsel.

I am blessed to have a mother who made the conscious decision to follow Christ before I was born, and did not waver in her faith in front of my siblings and me. My mother shared her past mistakes with my sisters and me, and always reminded us that we have the ability to make better choices and become great people.

Our parents' standards, limitations, or even accomplishments should not become our standards and limitations that we set for ourselves. As it is written in the Gospel according to John, "Very truly I tell you, whoever believes in me will do the works I have been doing, and they will do even greater things than these, because I am going to the Father. And I will do whatever you ask in my name, so that the Father may be glorified in the Son. You may ask me for anything in my name, and I will do it" (John 14:12–14).

The Lord's desire is that we make better decisions than the generations before us and that we achieve greater things than they did as well.

Chapter 7
Society Influences Our Choices

With just one push of a button we are instantly bombarded with information—some good, some useful, and some just bad for the soul. Throughout this book I mention the impact society has on the choices we make. Government, entertainers, even our community leaders can influence how we choose to live our lives. In these last days, it is important that we are not swayed by the world, but stand firm in what we believe to be true.

June 26, 2015, the White House was lit up in the colors of the rainbow to demonstrate the Supreme Court's ruling in favor of same-sex marriages. Nearly six months after the court's ruling, a bakery owner was ordered to pay a fine of $135,000 for refusing to bake a wedding cake for a same-sex couple. Edwin Meese once said, "A Supreme Court decision does not establish a 'supreme law of the land' that is binding on all persons and parts of government, henceforth and forevermore."

In no way am I trying to encourage anyone to break the law or go against our government officials, but I do encourage everyone that is reading this book to follow the law of one's conscience. As the apostle Paul writes in Romans, "They show that the requirements of the law are written on their hearts, their consciences also bearing witness, and their thoughts sometimes accusing them and at other times even defending them" (Rom. 2:15).

There have been countless stories of brave men and women who chose to stand up for what they believe in, even in the face of persecution. One story that comes to mind is the biblical story about three brave, young Jews named Meshach, Shadrach, and Abednego. All three men chose to stand up for what they believed, even if it would cost them their lives. When ordered to bow down and worship a gold statue, all three men refused because their religion had forbidden them to worship any god but their God.

"Furious with rage, Nebuchadnezzar summoned Shadrach, Meshach and Abednego. So these men were brought before the king, and Nebuchadnezzar said to them, 'Is it true, Shadrach, Meshach and Abednego, that you do not serve my gods or worship the image of gold I have set up? Now when you hear the sound of the horn, flute, zither, lyre, harp, pipe and all kinds of music, if you are ready to fall down and worship the image I made, very good. But if you do not worship it, you will be thrown immediately into a blazing furnace. Then what god will be able to rescue you from my hand?'

Shadrach, Meshach and Abednego replied to him, 'King Nebuchadnezzar, we do not need to defend ourselves before you in this matter. If we are thrown into the blazing furnace, the God we serve is able to deliver us from it, and he will deliver us from Your Majesty's hand. But even if he does not, we want you to know, Your Majesty, that we will not serve your gods or worship the image of gold you have set up'" (Dan. 3:13–18).

Making a decision that goes against societal norms is not easy, because the repercussions might be great, but sometimes the reward will be as well.

In the beginning of this chapter I mention that the entertainment industry can influence our decisions, probably not as directly as the government, but entertainment surely shapes our culture, values, and ideas. William Blake, an artist and poet, once said, "You become what you behold." The first time I read that statement I did not really think too much of it, until one day I was watching videos on YouTube and came across a video of a toddler watching a famous singer on TV, dancing and singing just like the singer he was watching. In that moment I realized the essence of the quote, "You become what you behold." The more we set our gaze on the things of this world, the more we will begin to think and reason as the world does.

An article in the NY Daily News titled, "Average American Watches Five Hours of TV per Day[4]" talks about the number of hours a week each age group watches television. The article states that those ages twelve to seventeen watch an average of twenty hours of TV a week, and young adults between the ages of eighteen and twenty-four watch about twenty-two hours. There have been numerous studies done about the impact TV has on the way we feel and think.

---

[4] Hinckley, David. "Average American watches 5 hours of TV per day." *NY Daily News*, NEW YORK DAILY NEWS, 5 Mar. 2014, www.nydailynews.com

When I was a youth director at the church I grew up in, I would always advise the youth to be aware of things they were watching and listening to. I knew that if they would change their gaze, they would be able to change their perspective and thus their choices. I would occasionally quote Colossians 3:2: "Set your minds on things above, not on earthly things." Understand that we were all created to be creative, and the entertainment industry can be an avenue to showcase our creativity; however, it should not be the source of our creativity.

The first day of every tutoring session, I have the students fill out a questionnaire so I can become better acquainted with them. One of the questions on the sheet asks the students what they want to be in the future. The answers are usually common occupations such as a teacher, nurse, or police officer. Occasionally I get students who want to be famous, a celebrity. When I ask them why, the students associate fame with wealth, beauty, and happiness. I must admit that I have been guilty of thinking famous people are all wealthy and happy. Famous actor Jim Carrey once said, "I think everybody should get rich and famous and do everything they ever dreamed of so they can see that it's not the answer."

It is so easy to believe that our society's standards are the right standards to live by, especially since we are constantly bombarded with information constructed by our society.

Even scientific research changes to fit modern culture, such as research done on drinking coffee and wine. A decade ago coffee was scientifically proven to cause health issues, but today it is considered healthy. Rules and laws evolve, changing how we feel and how we decide to make everyday choices. That is why I consider it so important to seek out the truth for myself. And what I have found is that Jesus Christ is the same, yesterday and today and forever. My faith is the standard I have chosen to base my decisions on, not society and its ever-changing ways.

Chapter 8
Ways Our Peers Influence Our Choices

Uniting with like-minded people can cause revolutionary things to happen. At an early age Bill Gates surrounded himself with friends who shared the same interest in computers and technology. Bill and his friend Paul Allen met each other while attending Lakeside School, a private High School in Seattle, Washington. The two young men developed a program called Traf-O-Data that helped show patterns of Seattle traffic. After graduating from Lakeside High, the two boys attended separate colleges but stayed in touch. Both Bill Gates and Paul Allen dropped out of college and later began working together at a company called Micro Instrumentation and Telemetry Systems (MITS). Soon after joining MITS the two men formed a partnership named Microsoft, which is now one of the largest companies in the world, making billions of dollars in profits every year.

You may have heard the expression, "Show me your friends and I will show you your future."

It is a powerful statement to suggest that my future is connected to the people I call friends. Most of us would say that our friends are like family; in fact, some might have closer relationships with friends than family, which is not a problem—as it is written in Proverbs 18:24, "But there is a friend who sticks closer than a brother."

Our friends' suggestions and advice can influence both trivial and important decisions we make. Just think about it: we ask our friends about what outfit to wear to a party, we want our friends' input on what college to attend, and we confide in our friends about marital problems. Our friends have a major impact on our decision making, which is why it is important to be selective when trying to get know other people.

Many books have been written on attracting and surrounding ourselves with positive people; however, more needs to be said on avoiding negative friendships and relationships. Most of us probably enter a relationship without thinking too much about how this person could hurt us, either because we believe their intentions are good or we simply don't care to know.

In 1 Corinthians 15:33 Paul writes, "Do not be misled: 'Bad company corrupts good character.'" A good friend is helpful in times of need, but a bad friend can literally ruin your life.

One of my students who lives in a group home for troubled teenage girls is energetic and funny and loves listening to hip-hop music. In one of our sessions her mood was different than usual. She seemed agitated and annoyed, which was not like her. She began to tell me that she did not want to be in the group home anymore. From the outside looking in, I truly believed that she was doing great, surrounded by people who care for her twenty-four hours a day. She told me that three friends of hers were admitted to the hospital the night before for trying to harm themselves. She was so frustrated while telling me this story because she felt as if these women thought it was some sort of joke the way it affected everyone else in the home.

It is almost impossible to go through life alone; you will need family and friends to help you, no doubt about that. However, be mindful of who you allow in your personal life, because people can change the trajectory of your future. "Walk with the wise and become wise, for a companion of fools suffers harm" (Prov. 13:20).

In one way or another we all have been victims of peer pressure, whether the influence was to help or harm us. Just think about how you spend your money. Growing up, my sisters and I really wanted to dress like our friends at school. The beginning of every school year we would make a list of all the outfits and shoes we wanted, and pray to God that we would find the money to buy them. And if we did get money, usually from family, we would spend all of it trying to look like our friends at school.

Peer pressure comes in many forms and can impact the choices we make. And note, not all pressure is bad; for instance, trying to get into a specific university because your friends are going can motivate you to perform well in school.

Open and honest relationships are healthy for growth and development. I don't think I would have made it through college if not for my friends who were with me when I had to pull all-nighters, or needed a shoulder to cry on. My friends and I shared our future goals and dreams with one another; we were all studying to be accountants. I did not feel an instant connection or immediately feel comfortable around my friends when we first met. I knew going into college that I should be careful who I shared my dreams with, because, unfortunately, not everyone may want the best for me.

The story of Joseph in the Bible comes to mind when thinking of people we consider to be friends or family, but who actually want to destroy your dreams. Joseph was one of Jacob's twelve sons. He did what was right, while his older brothers often did very wrong acts, which Joseph sometimes told their father. This made them very angry at Joseph. But they hated him still more because of two strange dreams he had. He told them, "Listen to this dream that I have dreamed. I dreamed that we were out in the field binding sheaves, when suddenly my sheaf stood up, and all your sheaves came around it and bowed down to my sheaf!" (Gen. 37:6–7). After hearing his dreams, his brothers plotted to kill Joseph, but decided to sell him into slavery instead.

Friends and family that do not share the same vision as you may find it difficult to support you. A good group of friends is really difficult to find, but is gratifying to have, even if the "group" is just you and someone else. C.S. Lewis once wrote, "The next best thing to being wise oneself is to live in a circle of those who are." Because whether you like it or not, you become like those you surround yourself with.

Part II
Ways We Can Make Better Choices

In Part I of this book we learned about factors that influence choices we make. In Part II we will explore ways to make better choices.

Statistics show that seven out of ten students walk away from their faith when they go to college. I believe that this is a result of young adults' freedom to finally make their own decisions in life. The freedom to act at one's own discretion, also known as free will, is both a beautiful and a dangerous gift. I would not want to trade my independence and freedom for anything, but every now and then I do appreciate my mother's stern advice and wisdom, as she still has the ability to help me avoid making mistakes. As mentioned earlier in this book, we all have the great power of free will and the power to choose what we want out of life—or to quote Uncle Ben, "With great power comes great responsibility."

For most of my life I have been involved in helping young adults realize their potential and worth in society. My passion for helping youth began when I was in college living with my younger sister and her three roommates. We lived in a four-bedroom apartment, and our neighbors across the hall were four guys attending the community college in town. I would occasionally invite the group of young men to our apartment for fellowship and game nights. Since I was the oldest person in the group, I would take the responsibility to facilitate the activities. At the end of every game night I would share a word of encouragement and a prayer. I remember one night before sending everyone on their way I told the group that I loved them and to have a good night. One of the guys who came that night was a friend of our neighbors; he looked at me and said, "Thank you. I never experienced something like this before."

From that moment I knew that I wanted to help young men and women experience true fellowship through Christ. And to teach them that it is through our choices that we can truly live the life that God has predestined for us. As with any relationship, our actions and decisions can either bring us closer together, or separate us from one another. This is also true of our relationship with God.

Chapter 9
Take the Leap of Faith

My once-in-a-lifetime opportunity came the morning of December 4, 2016, when I was lying on my bed and thought of something brilliant to write in my book, but did not write it down. Instead I just lay there until I fell asleep. You may be thinking that is really not a once-in-a-lifetime opportunity, but I would beg to differ with you. Because that forgotten thought may have led to a movement, been written into law, or changed someone's life. There have been plenty of times I could have taken a leap of faith into what seemed to be a once-in-a-lifetime moment, but I did not. I have read many stories of people choosing to do something radical in the hope of seeing their dreams come true, like quitting their job to pursue their passion in music or writing, or packing up everything to live in a new country. Whatever it is that is constantly pulling at you, take time to listen and respond.

My first real job after graduating college felt like a dream job. I worked for one of the top twenty CPA firms in America and got to travel to New York and other cities to audit Fortune 500 companies. I felt so accomplished and was sure there could not be a better job anywhere else for me, and I assumed my co-workers felt the same way. Well, I found that not all of them did.

While out on an auditing engagement, a co-worker and I began to talk about the University of Florida which we had both attended—the football games, the accounting courses, and our favorite professors. After a while our conversation became more personal. He shared with me his passion and what he actually wanted to do as a career. He showed me his tuna sandwich and asked if I wanted to try some. I politely declined but was definitely tempted. I never saw a tuna sandwich made like that before, with different peppers, chopped onions, and a mouthwatering aroma of zest and spices. He lit up when he began to talk about cooking for his family and girlfriend. My co-worker really wanted to be a chef and own his own restaurant, but instead he was sitting at a table with me, looking through files of paper. He was sure that this was the right path he had to take to his dream, which included $35,000 in student loans, pulling all-nighters studying for the CPA exam, and working years at a job that he hated. That was his choice. I can't say if it was the wrong or right choice, but it was definitely a costly and time-consuming path.

Taking a leap of faith can be a scary thing. I should know, because I am what most people might call risk averse. A risk averse person is reluctant to take risks. Most people think taking a risk involves jumping off a high building tied to a rope, or gambling all their money away in some shady investment.

Associating risk with dangerous activities would make anyone reluctant to take a risk. But for the purposes of this book, making a decision to take a risk or take a leap will have to start with first taking the leap of faith to make the decision to follow a Savior who will never fail you.

Two stories come to mind about taking a risk or leap of faith in the Bible. The first story is about a rich young ruler.

A young, rich man asked Jesus, "What good thing must I do to get eternal life?" (Matt. 19:16)

"And Jesus replied, "'You shall not murder, you shall not commit adultery, you shall not steal, you shall not give false testimony, honor your father and mother,' and 'love your neighbor as yourself.'"

"All these I have kept," the young man said. "What do I still lack?"

Jesus answered, "If you want to be perfect, go, sell your possessions and give to the poor, and you will have treasure in heaven. Then come, follow me." When the young man heard this, he went away sad, because he had great wealth" (Matt. 19:18–22).

Can you imagine someone telling you to give away everything you worked so hard for, to get closer to that person? Talk about risking it all. The rich, young ruler believed that his earthly wealth was more important than a relationship with Jesus.

The second Bible story that demonstrates people who chose to take a leap of faith is the story of Simon, who was also called Peter, and his brother Andrew. They chose to take a leap of faith when Jesus called out to them to follow Him.

"As Jesus was walking beside the Sea of Galilee, he saw two brothers; Simon called Peter and his brother Andrew. They were casting a net into the lake, for they were fishermen. 'Come, follow me,' Jesus said, 'and I will send you out to fish for people.' At once they left their nets and followed him" (Matt. 4:18–20).

Peter and Andrew were two of the twelve disciples that changed history by presenting Christianity to the nations. In both of the stories, each man was given the option to take a leap of faith and risk everything in the process. As the first two men to take the leap of faith and follow Jesus, the names of Peter and Andrew will always be remembered and repeated from one generation to the next, while the rich, young ruler's name has never been mentioned.

If anyone ever asked me the best decision I have made, I would simply say it was choosing to follow Jesus. There is no way I could have ever made any other wise decisions without my relationship with my heavenly Father. "It is because of him that you are in Christ Jesus, who has become for us wisdom from God— that is, our righteousness, holiness and redemption" (1 Cor. 1:30). Following Jesus saved me from a lot of mistakes I could have made.

It would be misleading to try to write a book about making better choices without including the One who has never made a mistake, a wrong choice, or committed any sin. Everything Jesus did on earth was for a purpose. Everything He said and did led to His ultimate purpose, which was to save humanity. The beginning of wisdom is to fear God and to know Him.

Chapter 10
Check Your Self

Growing up, my siblings and I often used the phrase, "Check yourself." By this we simply meant to analyze your heart, to make sure if you were being sincere about what you said or did in that moment. Whenever someone used the phrase in an argument, immediately you would notice the other person getting quiet for a moment to really take the time to check his or her motives. Often we focus on the "what" when making a decision. For example, we ask our friends, "What should I wear?" We ask our financial consultant what stocks to invest in. And we might ask close family members, "What should I do?"

I found that focusing more on the "why" instead of the "what" has brought me more clarity and has allowed me to make better choices in life. Asking yourself and others "Why?" allows you to check your motives (and the motives of others). Motive is defined as a reason for doing something, especially one that is hidden or not obvious.

I met my husband in college. He was an international student from Nigeria. I was born and raised in the great sunshine state of Florida with little knowledge about Africa except for what I have seen on TV. Within nine months of dating, my husband proposed to me, and it was such an exciting moment. I still remember waking my sisters and mother that night to tell them the good news. Everyone was so happy for me.

But after a while I began to ask myself why my husband wanted to marry me. Throughout our relationship I would occasionally ask him what was it that he loved about me, and he would say that I am good with kids, and that I was helpful. However, his answers never really made me entirely sure of his love for me because I did not know his motives—not until I began to ask the question why he loved me. Then his answers made me feel more secure. He said he loved my spirit and how I loved God, and how he imagined us growing old together. Then I knew that saying yes to him was the right decision, because I got to hear his heart and not so much of his logic.

Our motives can change over time, because the reality is that people are subject to change. Change is inevitable, meaning it is something we all must expect in each other and for ourselves. Our perspectives, desires, and understanding of life will constantly be evolving as we mature.

It saddens me to hear about people who may have started a career, a relationship, or a business with good motives and intentions, but later ended up committing fraud, cheating, or stealing. Working as an auditor I have heard surprising stories about organized crimes committed by ordinary people. One case involved an elderly woman who stole over $10,000 from a company that she had worked for, for more than twelve years, making me realize the impact our motives have on the choices we make. My senior manager described this woman as the sweetest woman he ever worked with, and never thought for one second that she could do something like this. But after her husband became ill, medical bills began piling up and she became desperate for extra cash. Her motive for stealing came from a place of desperation. Although she may have begun her career with good intentions, life's troubles changed her motives, thus affecting the choices she made.

It is not uncommon for people to do good with bad motives or do bad with good motives. The bottom line is, that if we search deep inside ourselves, we know the real reason why we do the things we do.

Our outward actions are a result of our inward thoughts and motives. Even good behavior can come from a place of bad intentions. "All a person's ways seem pure to them, but motives are weighed by the Lord" (Prov. 16:2).

In every major decision I have ever made, I took the time to evaluate and examine my heart. Every once in a while I take time out of my busy life to ask myself, "Why am I doing the things that I am doing, and what I am trying to achieve?" These questions help put things in perspective and keep me focused; and nine times out of ten my reason boils down to security.

Now it is easy for us to mistake security for wealth and money, which I have done plenty of times before. If I had a million dollars, then all my problems would go away, we think. Believing in the idea that money solves all problems, the majority of us enroll in college, pick the most lucrative major, and even try to surround ourselves with people above our societal class level so we can attain more money. Some might even undergo cosmetic procedures, or get involved in life-threatening jobs, or do illegal things, all for more money.

Scripture states that "the love of money is a root of all kinds of evil. Some people, eager for money, have wandered from the faith and pierced themselves with many griefs" (1 Tim. 6:10). And if money becomes your driving force, it will become your master. My mother used to say that money is a great servant but a terrible master.

"No one can serve two masters. Either you will hate the one and love the other, or you will be devoted to the one and despise the other. You cannot serve both God and money" (Matt. 6:24).

Unfortunately, many people motivated to attain wealth become servants to the very thing that was supposed to serve them.

"The purposes of a person's heart are deep waters, but one who has insight draws them out" (Prov. 20:5).

Our actions can stem from our lack of trust, selfish desires, or sincere love for others. Checking our motives should become a daily habit. It can be a checkpoint used to either allow us to go forward with a decision, or to stop us from making a terrible choice.

Chapter 11
Don't Rush

WAIT!—A word I heard my mother use all the time while growing up; whether it was yelled to my siblings and me, or said in a loving way, my mother knew the importance of waiting. She would quote the words of Solomon written in Ecclesiastes chapter 3, verse 1: "There is a time for everything, and a season for every activity under the heavens."

When making any decision in life, whether it's taking a leap of faith or deciding to enroll in a five-year Ph.D. program, it will happen in its appointed time. I have personally experienced the danger of rushing into an activity, a relationship, and a business opportunity several times.

One of my biggest struggles is patience. For example, whenever I read a book I flip through to see how many chapters I have left to read. And if I am at work I check the clock about every thirty minutes to see how much longer until it is time to go home. If you are anything like me, patience may not be your natural response when dealing with everyday life issues. However, patience is a virtue, and we have to be intentional about mastering patient behavior when making a decision.

I tell my students that life will always present the option to act now or to wait. The "act now" option can be described as "in the heat of the moment." That means engaging in an act while excited or angry, without taking the time to think about it. Don't get me wrong, there are times when making a decision in the heat of the moment is beneficial, like when a basketball player has only three seconds left in a game and throws the ball from half court, winning the championship. But most decisions made in the heat of the moment are detrimental and can leave us with lifelong consequences.

A typical example is a college freshman girl who finally gets to tell everyone she knows that she has a boyfriend. When left in her dorm room alone with the first boy to ever look at her the way Noah looked at Allie in the movie "The Notebook," she faces the option to act now or to wait.

The choice to wait might mean losing the boyfriend, but the choice to act now can lead to unwanted repercussions, such as an unwanted pregnancy (after a brief moment of pleasure). A young woman with an unplanned pregnancy faces an impossible decision between having an abortion (please note that an abortion is not the will of God; please seek help) or having the baby and probably dropping out of college. You do not have to rush. Slow down and think the whole thing through before acting.

No one said it would be easy to wait. In my season of waiting I noticed the time flies by if I occupy myself to get my mind off whatever it is I am waiting for. After I graduated with my bachelor's degree in December, 2012, I immediately began applying to graduate schools. I applied to three schools, and within two months I was rejected from two of them. The rejections were hard to take and began to make me worry about my last option and my future. Two more months went by, and the final school I had applied to still had not gotten back to me. I started to panic. I began making calls to the admissions office every day for about a week and was left with no answers. I was advised by the receptionist to check my online application for any notification. There were nights I could not sleep. Then one day I decided to go to the local book store and buy a book to read while I waited on the outcome of my application. That decision helped me to stop worrying about my acceptance letter. I can't really explain it, but as soon as I read the last page of that book, I went online to check my application and found out that I got ACCEPTED. Simply redirecting my energy on something positive helped me endure my season of waiting.

Please do not confuse waiting with procrastinating. Procrastination is an act to delay or postpone something. I must admit that there have been times that I missed great opportunities because I decided to procrastinate. English writer and social critic Charles Dickens once said, "Never do tomorrow what you can do today; procrastination is the thief of time." Procrastinating to start an assignment, a project, or a business task only delays your progress in accomplishing the goal you set for yourself.

Waiting does not mean we have to stop everything we are doing. I have friends who are waiting for a spouse, waiting to get married, or waiting to have a family, but while they wait they have gotten master's degrees, started careers, and traveled around the world. Do things that will edify you, and try not to compare your life to someone else's in your season of waiting. My point is that there is a time and season for everything, so don't rush. Take time to just enjoy the chapter you are reading, the chapter you are in now, and stop flipping to the end, because you might miss something good.

Chapter 12
Stop Comparing Yourself to Others

I have a confession to make: I am probably not the one who should be writing this chapter, as I have not yet mastered the art of contentment. Thank you Facebook and Instagram. Contentment is a state of being satisfied with the life you have been given. Before there were social media I had the dilemma of comparing myself to friends in my neighborhood and friends at my school. Thanks to social media I can now compare myself to millionaires living around the world (who do not know I exist). I have spent countless hours pressuring my husband to try to make our lives resemble what I see on social media. Fortunately for me, my husband has the wisdom to remind me that life happens in stages and we should be content with the stage we are in now.

Many people have put themselves in debt trying to keep up with someone else's standard of living: buying houses and cars they cannot afford, going on vacations that are way out of their budget, and getting plastic surgery to try to fit in. If you are anything like me, and make choices by comparing yourself to others, the truth is that you might not be living the most authentic and fulfilled life you could be enjoying.

From the outside looking in, most people might look like they have it all together, with a picture-perfect life (again, thank you social media). However, in reality, we all have issues, we will all go through life's challenges, and there is just no escaping it.

"I have told you these things, so that in me you may have peace. In this world you will have trouble. But take heart! I have overcome the world" (John 16:33).

I once heard someone say that many people want the blessings of someone else but they ignore the pain, struggles, and hardship that person may have endured to get to a place of happiness, success, or peace. Everyone wants to play basketball like Michael Jordan, but they don't want to practice like him. Most may want the wealth of Warren Buffet, but they may not want to make the same sacrifices he made.

Now do not get me wrong: it is perfectly fine to get inspired by someone else's success and achievement. I do it all the time. I get inspired to eat healthier and work out more whenever I look at fitness models on the internet. There is information that others may know that you are trying to learn, and social media has created a platform to share valuable information. However, there is a thin line between inspiration and envy. How do I know? Because I have fallen victim to it.

Marriage is exciting and brings a lot of joy, but sometimes things can become so routine that you forget to make time to have fun. I began to look for new and fresh ideas to share with my husband. I began to follow this one married couple who seemed to be truly enjoying each other's company as they went on dates and lavish vacations. At first it was once a week, but after a while I began to check in on this couple's page twice a day to see if they posted anything new. This minor obsession began to affect my marriage as I would constantly compare my husband to the one I was watching on social media. "We do not dare to classify or compare ourselves with some who commend themselves. When they measure themselves by themselves and compare themselves with themselves, they are not wise" (2 Cor. 10:12).

It's never a good idea to make choices on the basis of comparing yourself to someone else. The truth is, you never really know all there is to know about an individual, their thoughts, their heart, their struggles, the good and the bad. If you knew, I am sure you would be a little more confident in who God created you to be.

Chapter 13
Look at the Big Picture

A magnifying glass is a tool used to enlarge an image of an object. For the majority of my life I have made decisions by emphasizing or enlarging minor things instead of looking at the bigger picture. My wedding day was one of the scariest, yet most exciting, times in my life. I had almost everything ready and prepared to walk down the aisle to the man of my dreams—except for my veil. The day I purchased my wedding dress, I was given the option to get a veil at a discount price but did not see one I liked. Days went by and I still had not found a veil that I felt was worthy enough for my dress. On the morning of my wedding I began to panic at the thought of walking down the aisle without a veil. I was willing to do anything and pay any price to find one. I thought about going back to the bridal store to purchase the $200 veil (which I really did not like and was way out of my budget), but then my mother told me about a small dress store nearby that sold veils for a very decent price. I went to the smaller bridal store, and within five minutes I walked out with a $25 veil.

In that moment I realized that a wedding is bigger than the ring, the dress, the shoes, and yes, the veil. I decided that I was not going to waste money on something so insignificant. I chose instead to look at the big picture, which was the actual marriage, a new journey with another soul, rather than worry about a five-hour event.

Our future is the big picture. It is the picture we should look at when making everyday decisions, much like the picture on a box of a jigsaw puzzle. Every choice we make is a small piece of a puzzle that will eventually form a picture, the picture of our future.

Occasionally I ask my students, "What kind of future do you want to have, and why?" This question allows them to have the end goal in mind. And I will then ask what they are doing today to make the future they want become a reality.

Growing up poor, I decided very early that I was not going to stay poor and that my kids were going to have a better life than I did. I knew that I did not have the same opportunities that many of the wealthy kids in America have, like their parents' connections and money. My only way out was through education, which I took very seriously. I remember in high school when all my friends were at a pep rally for homecoming, I was in the guidance counselor's office using her computer so I could apply for scholarships. There were many things I had to forego to get into the college I wanted, and let's just say it is great to be a Florida Gator! My circumstances at the time did not make me lose focus on the ultimate goals, nor did my past.

Our past has a way of making our future seem a bit blurry; it can get in the way of where we are trying to go. A guest speaker came to speak one Saturday morning at the church my husband and I attend. This guest speaker had spoken at our church several times before, and I really enjoyed his talks. He is of Greek descent and speaks with passion and authority, his presence and demeanor demanding the attention of his audience. On this Saturday morning he spoke in a much different way than usual, and was a bit more open and vulnerable. He shared how his past affected his future choices. When he was a young boy he was molested, a secret he kept from friends and family. Although he held this terrible secret, he still managed to make something of himself. He got a law degree, got married, and started a business. When his business began to thrive he considered running for office, becoming the governor of the state where he lived, but he decided not to run because of his past. He worried that if he ran for office, people might find out what happened to him as a young boy. As I watched him share his story, I couldn't stop my tears from rolling down my face; when I looked at this speaker I saw only greatness and wisdom, but when he looked in the mirror he saw shame and abuse.

There are so many people who let their past get in the way of the bigger picture, which is a great future. I often hear women say they are not worthy enough to have anything good because of their past mistakes and choices. It is written in Scripture, "Forget the former things; do not dwell on the past. See, I am doing a new thing! Now it springs up; do you not perceive it? I am making a way in the wilderness and streams in the wasteland" (Isa. 43:18–19).

You may have heard the expression, "Don't let your past dictate your future." This idea is valuable and should be taken seriously. Our future is what we should look forward to, and we should make an effort to do everything we can to have the future we desire.

At least once a week I like to jog about a mile from my house. I feel more energetic, alert, and healthy after I exercise. However, I must admit, I do not always look forward to my run. Sometimes I even dread it, but I know the benefits of exercising, and that is why I do it: for the end results and all the benefits. I usually begin running with a lot of energy and momentum. I sometimes run with music, and will start with a good pace, but after a while my breathing becomes heavier and I begin to jog more slowly. I mentally encourage myself to keep going and force myself to keep running. It never fails that every time I get close to my house, it becomes the hardest to keep going. When I am close to the finish line, I feel the most pressure to just give up and start walking.

This is pretty much how all of my major accomplishments felt—finishing school, then grad school, passing the state board exam to become a CPA, and writing this book—the end of the process always felt the hardest to get through. The apostle Paul writes in Philippians chapter 3, "Brothers and sisters, I do not consider myself yet to have taken hold of it. But one thing I do: Forgetting what is behind and straining toward what is ahead, I press on toward the goal to win the prize for which God has called me heavenward in Christ Jesus" (Phil. 3:13–14).

We all start this life as an artist with a blank canvas. With each stroke of paint, or with every choice we make, we create the picture that the world will soon remember. How do you want the picture of your life to look? When you find the answer to the question, begin painting the masterpiece of your life. Don't stop or quit along the way, but keep painting until you reach your goal.

Chapter 14
Seek Advice

Whenever I make a decision resulting in an unfavorable outcome, I notice I made that decision usually on my own, without seeking help. In Proverbs it says that "the way of fools seems right to them, but the wise listen to advice" (Prov. 12:15). It's dangerous to believe that we can go through life on our own strength and wisdom, but unfortunately many of us try to do just that. What hurts me the most about mentoring young adults is to look into their eyes, when I ask, "Is everything okay?" and to see them look back at me with obvious doubt and uncertainty there, but hear them reply, "Yes, I'm fine."

I remember a conversation I had with one of the youths after the service back at my home church. Earlier that day I had shared with the youth how important it is to ask for help. Immediately after the service, one of the youth came up to me and began talking to me about my message. Knowing this young lady, I knew she wasn't there just to tell me how much she enjoyed the sermon. She looked like she was holding a secret and wanted to ask for help. So I began to make light conversation, and immediately she interrupted me to ask who to talk to, who to ask for help. Without any hesitation, I said you can talk to me and the other youth leaders. But she just said, "Okay," and walked away. I'm not sure why she didn't talk to me that day, but honestly, at the time, I must admit that I was afraid to hear what she might have to say. I watched this young girl grow up right in front of me, and I viewed her as an angel that was headed in the right direction. So to hear her ask me that question took me by surprise, and I think she noticed. And I think that's where the problem lies: the fear of being judged whenever we ask for help.

This problem is not a young adult problem, it's a universal problem. People refuse to seek help for fear of being judged. After my encounter with the young lady, I began to analyze my behavior and reaction whenever I spoke at youth meetings. I wanted to show a more relaxed demeanor in the hope that they would feel comfortable to talk to me about things they might not want to discuss with their parents. My approach began to work, and I realized that underneath this "I know it all" persona most of us create, deep down inside we all are waiting for someone to talk to and help us navigate the sea of life.

My older sister has always had a pessimistic view on life (she has gotten better). She would tell my siblings and me that not everyone is for you and to be careful who you confide in. It's true that not everyone wants the best for you. What is difficult about this statement is trying to figure out who is on your side. Seeking help and asking for advice is not easy, because it means we have to allow ourselves to become vulnerable. And unfortunately there are people that will prey on others' vulnerability for reasons I can't really explain.

King David knew how it felt to be betrayed by someone he once confided in: "If an enemy were insulting me, I could endure it; if a foe were rising against me, I could hide. But it is you, a man like myself, my companion, my close friend, with whom I once enjoyed sweet fellowship at the house of God, as we walked about among the worshipers" (Psalms 55:12–14).

Betrayal can lead to mistrust in others and cause someone to shut everyone out, which I have found can be very dangerous. There is a real enemy out there, and his mission is to steal, kill, and destroy. The first tactic the enemy uses to accomplish his mission is isolation. It is easy for us to feel like we are alone, like we are the only person going through whatever we may be going through, but it's not true. I am not alone, you are not alone, we are not alone, and the truth is, we need each other.

I am fortunate to have a mother who I can be open and honest with about everything. She has helped me navigate through some of my darkest moments, and I do not think I would be who I am today without her wisdom and support. Unfortunately, not everyone has a good relationship with their parents. The only thing I can write about this matter is to pray about it. Growing up I would seek my mother's advice before making any big decision; now I seek my husband's advice. And when there were times my mother wasn't available, I would seek advice from the other older people, either at my place of work or in my church. An older person has wisdom and knows things that at our age we cannot know because we have not yet experienced it. Their counsel is very important. Nonetheless, good advice can come from someone of any age; just be careful to take advice that aligns with what you believe.

Chapter 15
Keep Choosing the Right Way Until it Becomes a Natural Response

There are many ways to define success and accomplishment in life. For me success is someone excelling and growing in his or her passion, whether it be in business, the fine arts, or ministry. Some might weigh success with a monetary scale, while others weigh it with the number of people they influence. My point is that not everyone wants the same thing, so it will be inaccurate to define what the right choice or what the wrong choice is.

At a youth Bible study in my home church, I urged all of the youth to go to college and get a degree. I told them that they should reach for the stars and never let anyone tell them that they can't be a doctor, nurse, lawyer, teacher, or the next president of the United States. A couple days after that Bible study meeting, I ran into one of the youth, and he was so excited to tell me his dreams and aspirations. Knowing this young man, I was sure he was going to say he wanted to go into politics, but he surprised me by saying he was looking at culinary schools. Puzzled, I said, "That's great," and then I remembered my speech. Not once did I mention chef as a career choice, because truthfully I did not regard it as such. But in that moment, looking at how excited he was, I realized we all have different goals in life, so therefore our choices will be different as well, which is okay.

For the purpose of this book, I want to emphasize that choosing the right way is more of an internal decision that impacts our external lives. There is no way I can tell anyone what is the right career, the right school to attend, or the right person to date, because I am in no position to make such a decision for another person. The right choice is what Paul speaks of when he writes in Romans chapter 7 about his struggle to do good:

"I do not understand what I do. For what I want to do I do not do, but what I hate I do. And if I do what I do not want to do, I agree that the law is good. As it is, it is no longer I myself who do it, but it is sin living in me. For I know that good itself does not dwell in me, that is, in my sinful nature. For I have the desire to do what is good, but I cannot carry it out.

For I do not do the good I want to do, but the evil I do not want to do—this I keep on doing. Now if I do what I do not want to do, it is no longer I who do it, but it is sin living in me that does it."

The struggle to do good, to choose the right thought, the right attitude, and the right behavior is a struggle we all face in one way or another. I remember the day my twin sister and I first stole candy from a store. I can still remember how scared I was, how my heart was beating so fast in my chest, how it took forever to get to the door. As soon as I made it out of the store I felt such relief that we didn't get caught. Needless to say, that was not our last shoplifting trip we made to that store. Stealing candy became less scary every time we did it; it began to not feel so wrong to me anymore. Fortunately for us, we did end up getting caught when my sister hid some candy under her armpits and was asked by the cashier to lift her arms. That was probably one of the most heart-wrenching days of my life; I was around ten years old at the time.

This is how sin operates: the first time it feels so wrong, so dirty, just not right, but after a while it begins to feel normal, even to point that we may justify it as right. Conscious refers to "an individual sense of recognition of something within or without oneself," or it can mean "painfully aware of; sensitive to." I include the second definition because whenever I knowingly make a bad decision or choose the wrong thing to do, it's a painful experience for me—not so much physically, but mentally and spiritually.

A conversation I once had with a friend back in college turned out to be the most open and honest conversation I ever had with someone other than family. Her dorm room was two doors down from mine. We would occasionally see each other in the kitchen area, where we would talk for hours. She grew up as the only child of a divorced mother. She did not affiliate herself with any religion, but was open and accepting of everyone's religious beliefs. She would confide in me and tell me how she felt attracted to other women, and I would ask her where such feelings came from. She would try to explain it to me but never really knew the answer. She told me she dated all types of men and enjoyed the physical relationships she had with them, but she wanted to experience what it would be like to be with a woman. I told her that it wasn't right, that the feelings she was having could stem from another source and that she shouldn't indulge in such thoughts. A couple of weeks after our conversation, we met again in the kitchen. She told me that she had been with a woman and the experience was awful. She deeply regretted it. I did not know what to say. I will never forget the look she gave me; it was as if she had lost something she could never get back. We never really spoke again after that.

I could not help but wonder why she would feel regret if she had never been told that action was wrong. Her mother raised her to find her own happiness in whatever form it came, so why did she feel so terrible if that is what she wanted?

Many people believe that the only acts that are truly wrong are the obvious ones like stealing, cheating, and killing. But Paul writes in Romans chapter 3 verse 20, "Therefore no one will be declared righteous in God's sight by the works of the law; rather, through the law we become conscious of our sin."

It's our conscience that lets us know we have done something wrong or against the will of God. My mother would tell me, "If you hear that small voice in the back of your head telling you something is wrong, then it's wrong, and thank God you have the Holy Spirit operating in you." The real question is, will you listen to that still, small voice and deny yourself? We all are born sinners, with impure thoughts and desires, but we must deny ourselves daily if we want to seek truth. Jesus spoke to His disciples saying, "Whoever wants to be my disciple must deny themselves and take up their cross daily and follow me" (Luke 9:23).

But what if I don't feel any remorse or regret when I engage in an activity that some might view as wrong? This is a question I've been asked many times. It would be naive to believe that we are all wired the same, with the same thoughts and emotions. For instance, my husband is the more rational one in our relationship; he looks at the facts and concrete details, while I try to connect emotionally. So whenever I try to explain anything to my husband, I use less emotional talk and more logical reasoning to get my point across.

The apostle Paul also addresses those of us who might need to be convinced in a more logical a way when he writes, "Everything is permissible but not everything is beneficial" (1 Cor. 10:23).

The majority of us can do almost anything we want; we have the means, the technology, and the resources to do so. However, that does not mean we should take advantage of that freedom.

Choosing the right thing to do may not come naturally for many of us, especially if we have not seen it modeled in front of us. For example, eating healthy does not come naturally to me. Growing up, my siblings and I would skip out on church to go eat at the nearest McDonald's. We would use all the money we had saved the prior week and spend it all on burgers and fries. Oh those fries, every time we would go to McDonald's I would say a silent prayer hoping the fries would be hot and sprinkled with just the right amount of salt.

Eating healthy was a conscious decision I had to make. Now, I enjoy eating fruits and salads. It took many years of choosing the healthier option to allow it to become a natural craving, or habit, but nonetheless, I am glad I kept choosing the right things to eat. Don't get me wrong, there have been times when I backslid, but thank God for His grace. "I will heal their backsliding, I will love them freely: for mine anger is turned away from him" (Hosea 14:4.KJV).

Maybe your eating habits are not a problem. When making poor choices, it could be choosing the same type of friends that continue to lead you astray, or making the same relationship mistake with every person you date.

Choosing to become a better version of yourself will require sacrifices. You may lose friendships along the way, lose money, or lose out on opportunities that may have appeared to be great, but in reality were not worth losing yourself. Whatever your struggle may be, remember it's never too late to start making the right choice, and keep making the right choice, until it becomes a natural response.

Chapter 16
Be Mindful of Others

It is a misconception to believe that our choices affect only us, personally. But something as simple and individualistic as buying chocolate or coffee from a local coffee shop will impact so many people, all in different ways. To think like this may be a bit overwhelming, but if we can develop a habit to think of others, we might make different choices.

My pastor in Gainesville practiced the principle of being mindful of others. He would occasionally tell the congregation that he and his family stopped buying chocolate from large manufacturing companies because of how those companies are involved in child slavery. Chocolate is made from cocoa beans, which are grown in many West African countries, such as Côte d'Ivoire, Ghana, and Cameroon. In recent years non-profit organizations and news reporters have exposed the widespread use of child labor on cocoa bean farms. Many began to protest large chocolate manufacturing companies by boycotting their product if they did not change their labor laws. Sadly, child labor has actually increased since the first article was published. My pastor felt passionate about the issue, and made the decision not to buy any chocolate from certain companies. His bold act of passion for children in Africa and around the world actually began to cause a ripple effect. The University of Florida students who attended his church began to protest chocolate as well, and urged their friends to do so, too.

We may not be aware of the ripple effect our choices and actions have on others around us, but our choices do impact others. This effect is especially seen if someone has a leadership position. Before you say, "Well, I'm not in any leadership position," you might be, in more ways than you realize. I am the seventh child and have three younger siblings, so I am very careful of my actions, always trying to set a good example for my younger sisters and brother.

Most of the people who influenced me were friends and family who did not have an important title behind their name, just some "good ol'" wisdom. In high school, I was known as the newspaper geek with the outspoken, cool twin sister. I did not realize that my teachers and peers were observing me, until one day I was caught kissing my boyfriend in the hallway. My teacher walked over and said, "I am shocked; this is not like you." My teacher's statement took me by surprise because I was not sure what he meant by that, but then I remembered some of the discussions we had in his classroom. He was always so intrigued and delighted in the ways I would present my arguments while defending my faith, which must have left an impression on him even though he was an atheist. The point I am trying to get across is that we all are influencing someone in one way or another, even if we are not aware of it.

Being mindful of others is not just about how your actions and choices might influence people around you. It is really about thinking of others before thinking about yourself. Most of us ask the question, "How will this benefit me?" I believe this is a reasonable question to ask. But don't just stop at that. Also ask yourself how this will benefit others. My husband once said that in helping others you are actually helping yourself. In Philippians it says, "Do nothing out of selfish ambition or vain conceit. Rather, in humility value others above yourselves, not looking to your own interests but each of you to the interests of the others" (Phil. 2:3–4).

This is difficult, especially when others might not share your values. Our generation is somewhat in the "me" era, an era when it is normal to be consumed by one's own ambitions, interests, and welfare.

Research has found that this generation, despite all of the technological advancements, is more isolated than previous generations. Nowadays someone can have 1.2 million followers on Instagram, 2.3 million subscribers on YouTube, and over a thousand Facebook friends, but still feel lonely because of the lack of actual physical connection.

When I was young, I would occasionally hear my mother and her church friends talk about how different life was when they were growing up. She would stress the idea of community—something my generation seems to have lost. She would tell us how her neighbors would watch after her and my aunt and uncle (my mother's siblings), whenever my grandparents had to step out. Each kid in the neighborhood was the child of every adult in the community. Someone's loss and misfortune became the loss and misfortune of the entire community; joys and accomplishments were similarly shared. Unity is what came to mind when my mother spoke about how life was for her when she was growing up. The generation before us was not perfect by any means, but they knew the power of unity.

There is an old African proverb that says, "If you want to go quickly, go alone, but if you want to go far, go together." My understanding of this proverb is that we need one another to achieve our goals. Some have used this proverb to describe the benefits of marriage, saying "two heads are better than one."

In the world of business I have seen people use others selfishly as a stepping stone to reach their own personal goals. Using others and being used is not good and it is not fair; I know this from experience. The point is, it is good to think of the benefits of others. One of the greatest commandments is to love your neighbor as yourself. This commandment emphasizes the importance of thinking about others in the same way you would think about yourself. It is with this attitude that great leaders, thinkers, and innovators have impacted so many people.

President John F. Kennedy once said, "The rights of every man are diminished when the rights of one man are threatened." We are our brother's keeper, and if we are able to think as such, we will be able to make better choices, not just for ourselves but for everyone around us.

Chapter 17
Learn from Past Mistakes and Experiences

We all make mistakes; that is a fact. No one is perfect, and no matter how hard you may try to do everything right, life has a way of letting you know how wrong you are. The worst thing you can do is to go against life's lessons and continue making the same mistake over and over again. Albert Einstein once said, "Insanity is doing the same thing over and over again and expecting different results."

I watched my friend go from one relationship to the next with guys that were all close friends, and saw her get hurt time after time. I couldn't believe that she actually expected one relationship to be different from the last, when she was dating the same type of guys. I tried to make sense of why someone repeatedly makes the same mistake over and over, and then I thought about my own stubborn behaviors. I never really had a major problem with relationship mistakes; in fact, I was so afraid of disappointment that I rarely dated, just to reduce my chances of getting hurt.

No, my insanity involved failing to follow my passion wholeheartedly. I mentioned that I am a certified public accountant, but the truth is that it took a lot of effort to become certified, and to be honest, I do not believe that this is what I am called to do. I believe I was called to do what I am doing right now: write. For a long time I kept ignoring and pushing my passion for writing to the side, while chasing the wind, whatever that might be. After being fired not once, but twice, I realized that I finally had to make a decision to pursue my passion for writing. In the midst of failure and making mistakes, I realized I had to make a change.

Now there is a difference between not giving up after failing a couple of times, and knowing when it's time to make a change, and it is important that we can tell the difference. Scholars say it took Thomas Edison about a thousand failed attempts to make the first successful light bulb, one of the most important inventions in history. Edison kept learning more from each failed attempt and persisted until he got it right.

There will be times to keep going in one direction even when it seems difficult, and there will be times to change the direction you are on; it is up to each individual to know the difference.

Every new decision we make should consider the previous choices we have made in our past. A member from my church shared his testimony of how he decided to stop drinking alcohol. At a very young age he began drinking with his friends from school, and as he grew up and went off to college he began drinking even more at parties and other social events. One night after partying he got into an accident in which his car flipped over; however, he walked away without a scratch. Now every time he is offered a drink he politely declines because he remembers that potentially fatal night that God showed him grace.

Growth and development do not happen overnight, and it is not a straight path, but every step should be better than the last, and every generation should be better than the previous. We can only accomplish this by learning from our past mistakes and failures.

Final Chapter
God's Grace

Who am I? I honestly I ask myself that question all the time. I was conceived and born in sin; nothing about me is perfect. Please let that disclaimer seep deep into the back of your mind. I am who I am because of God's grace. I have made many poor choices in my life, and time after time God's grace has covered me. For a long time I believed if I did everything right, and made all the right decisions, that I would be successful and live a good life. Big mistake, because I thought I could do it all on my own, with my own strength, wisdom, and self-discipline. Boy was I wrong.

When I was younger I used to look down on leaders who fell into temptation. I was the first to cast my stone at such leaders until I got older and realized that "all have sinned and fall short of the glory of God" (Rom. 3:23). If anyone is thriving, living a life that is worthy to praise, it is only by the grace of God and His unfailing love. Please understand my hope is that everyone who reads this book will try to be more conscious of the impact their choices have on their lives, but most importantly, the impact God's grace has on each of our lives. It is only by His grace that we are saved.

I have been fortunate enough to travel to different countries and see firsthand that not everyone in life is given the same opportunities. My first trip to Haiti after the devastating 2010 earthquake awakened a deep sorrow in me. I questioned God's sovereignty and asked how God could allow anyone to go through so much pain and loss. One Sunday morning, as I walked through the streets of Haiti, I heard the most beautiful sound of worship coming from a room in an old, unkempt building. At that moment I remembered that "weeping may stay for the night, but rejoicing comes in the morning" (Psalms 30:5).

I may not know all there is to know about God, but I know His love for humankind is unconditional and unwavering. And it is through grace that I have come to know the love of God. Grace has been described as a gift that has been freely given to humankind, a gift that cannot be earned. This grace has kept me from making choices that could have ended my life, choices that could have caused me to lose everything and everyone I love. While we cannot choose all the things that happen to us, we can choose to live, and to live a purposeful life with love and truth.

I believe our purpose in life is to lift one another up. Choosing to live a life filled with purpose does not mean you will make no mistakes along the way. The truth is, no one is perfect. We all are sinners; we all have made choices in life that should have resulted in the death penalty, but thank God for His grace.

Consider the adulterous woman who was brought out to be stoned to death by her community. Jesus saved her life by saying to the crowd, "Let any one of you who is without sin be the first to throw a stone" (John 8:7). In that moment, Jesus made the crowd—and every believer—realize that we all have sinned, we all have failed one time or another in making the right decision, but we all can get back up. As Jesus instructed the woman, "Go now and leave your life of sin." God's grace is sufficient, but the choice whether to live in His grace or live a life of sin is a choice we have to make daily.

I will never forget the words of a woman who I tried to minister to on the streets. My husband and I were holding signs that people could read and ask us questions, which we would answer with encouraging words from the Bible. This one lady stopped to read our sign and moments later began to pour out her soul to us. She first told us how thrilled she was to see young people so passionate about the Lord, and then she began to share her upbringing and all the trials she had been through. At the end of our conversation she said, "I wish I had chosen to follow Christ sooner in my youth, like you." Her words reminded me of a quote Oprah Winfrey once said: "Life with few regrets is a life well lived."

My hope is that this book will inspire you to make choices that will bring the most joy and peace to your life while you are still young, so you can reap the harvest it will bring in the future.

References

1. "choice n.1.". In Oxford English dictionary. Retrieved from https://en.oxforddictionaries.com/definition/choice

2. Wikipedia contributors. "Choice." Wikipedia, The Free Encyclopedia. Wikipedia, The Free Encyclopedia, 16 Jun. 2017. Web.

5 Sep. 2017

3. "Martin Luther King, Jr. Quotes." BrainyQuote.com. Xplore Inc, 2017. 5 September 2017. https://www.brainyquote.com/quotes/quotes/m/martinluth103571.html

4. Wikipedia contributors. "Political correctness." Wikipedia, The Free Encyclopedia. Wikipedia, The Free Encyclopedia, 15 Aug. 2017. Web.

5 Sep. 2017

5. History.com Staff. "SENECA FALLS CONVENTION BEGINS." History.com, A E Networks, 2010, www.history.com/this-day-in-history/seneca-falls-convention-begins.

6. Intimidate n.3 (2017, August 16). In Dictionary.com Retrieved from

http://www.dictionary.com/browse/intimidating?o=10007

7. Oxford Essential Quotations, Edited by Susan Ratcliffe, Entry: Alex Hamilton, Publisher Oxford University Press, Oxford Reference Online, Published online: 2012, Online Version: 2013, (Accessed February 18, 2014

8. "Bill Johnson." AZQuotes.com. Wind and Fly LTD, 2017. 05 September 2017. http://www.azquotes.com/quote/1318692

9. Wikipedia contributors. "Self-esteem." Wikipedia, The Free Encyclopedia. Wikipedia, The Free Encyclopedia, 27 Sep. 2017. Web. 5 Oct. 2017

10. Kaptein, Muel, Why Do Good People Sometimes Do Bad Things?: 52 Reflections on Ethics at Work (July 25, 2012). Available at SSRN: https://ssrn.com/abstract=2117396 or http://dx.doi.org/10.2139/ssrn.2117396

11. Winch, Guy. "5 Ways Emotional Pain Is Worse Than Physical Pain." Psychology Today, Sussex Publishers, 20 July 2014, www.psychologytoday.com/blog/the-squeaky-wheel/201407/5-ways-emotional-pain-is-worse-physical-pain.

12. Lo, Em &. "How Many Sexual Partners Is Too Many?" The Huffington Post, TheHuffingtonPost.com, 24 Mar. 2016, www.huffingtonpost.com/em-and-lo/how-many-sexual-partners-is-too-many_b_9542296.html.

13. Hinckley, David. "Average American watches 5 hours of TV per day." NY Daily News, NEW YORK DAILY NEWS, 5 Mar. 2014, www.nydailynews.com/life-style/average-american-watches-5-hours-tv-day-article-1.1711954.

14. "Motive | Definition of motive in US English by Oxford Dictionaries." Oxford Dictionaries | English, Oxford Dictionaries, en.oxforddictionaries.com/definition/us/MOTIVE.

www.ingramcontent.com/pod-product-compliance
Lightning Source LLC
Chambersburg PA
CBHW022120040426
42450CB00006B/778